TIME
FOR KIDS
READERS

Goods
AROUND THE WORLD

by Susan Ring

**Harcourt**

Orlando   Austin   Chicago   New York   Toronto   London   San Diego

Visit *The Learning Site!*
www.harcourtschool.com

We shop in stores. Some of the things that we buy come from the United States. Other things that we buy come from far away.

AUSTRALIA

Wool comes from sheep. Some sheep live in Australia.

3

We eat bananas. Sometimes they come from Brazil. Brazil is in South America.

ATLANTIC OCEAN

PACIFIC OCEAN

BRAZIL

Rice grows in big, wet fields in Asia. After the grain is grown and cut, it is sent around the world. This rice field is in Indonesia.

ASIA

PACIFIC OCEAN

INDONESIA

Mexico ships a lot of silver to the United States.

MEXICO

UNITED STATES

ATLANTIC OCEAN

PACIFIC OCEAN

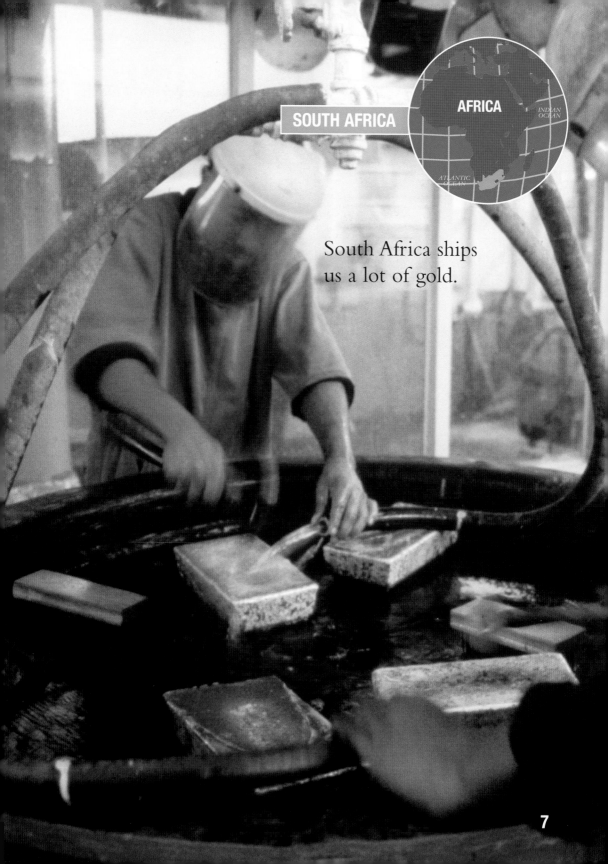

SOUTH AFRICA

AFRICA

INDIAN OCEAN

ATLANTIC OCEAN

South Africa ships
us a lot of gold.

Even the gas in your car may have come from a place far away.